SCHOOL

OF

THE

PROPHETS

A PROPHETIC TRAINING
STUDENT MANUAL

MICHELLE COLE MINISTRIES

APOSTLE MICHELLE COLE

Dear Student,

I would like to personally welcome you and thank you for considering the Prophetic Training that is offered through Michelle Cole Ministries, a nondenominational ministry that is dedicated to serving the Body of Christ. Your interest in understanding prophetic ministry, spiritual gifting, and the office of a prophet will be taught with Biblical Revelation.

School of the Prophets is open to all who desire a clear understanding of the prophetic, to grow in the ministry gift and the office of a prophet, and to also grow right where you are at, whatever you are called to be in the Body of Christ. Pastors and other church leaders who are seeking an increased release of the prophetic anointing in their local congregation are strongly encouraged to participate.

Michelle Cole Ministries offers a Certificate of Completion to everyone that completes all classes. Ordination upon completion is available for **membership only.** All students are welcome to enroll.

Walking in His authority,

Apostle Michelle Cole

CONTENTS

ACKNOWLEDGEMENTS

I would like to thank Jeremiah, Elijah, and Elisha for your thoughts, prayers, and support. You all are wonderful sons. I thank God for each of you.

I would like to thank Chief Apostle Israel Jones, Sr., Overseer Shirley Elms, and the late Pastor Ruthie L. Hudson for being great leaders and for playing a major role in my life. I thank each of you for your wisdom, guidance, and prayers.

I would like to thank Pastor Yolanda Nickerson for helping bring my new book to fruition.

I would like to thank Star Photography for your great work.

INTRODUCTION

In this season of your life, your desire to be developed in the area of prophecy and understand the gift of prophecy and the office of the prophet will be fulfilled. I have put together some tools, resources, and research of information in this manual. The Holy Spirit has given me teaching strategies and revelation to effectively teach and impart in the Prophetic Training.

The Prophetic Training is designed to build the members of the Body of Christ. Every gift in the Fivefold Ministry is a **power gift** from God, because they all connect to faith, miracles, and healings, though the gifts function differently. The Fivefold Ministry consists of apostles, prophets, evangelists, pastors, and teachers. Read Ephesians 4:11.

The information shared in this manual will be beneficial to everyone. There is often an element of intimidation in the church community when it comes to the office of a prophet or the gift of prophecy being exercised. This manual will help spiritual leaders, praise and worship leaders, and all other ministries to understand the prophetic and how to flow in that capacity. There are streams of flow in the prophetic.

What is School of the Prophets?

School of the Prophets provides a setting for spiritual experiences, edification, impartation, and activations, and a space to have in-depth discussions of biblical principles to impart in each student. The revelation wisdom given to me by God and the Holy Spirit to share with others to be a conduit to open portals in the realm of the spirit, so that access will be opened to His will.

1 Samuel 19:20 (KJV)—**CALLED THEM A "COMPANY OF PROPHETS."**

"And Saul sent messengers to take David, and when they saw the company of prophets prophesying, and Samuel standing as appointed over them, the Spirit of God was upon the messengers of Saul, and they also prophesied." -1 Samuel 19:20-24 (KJV).

2 Kings 2:3 (KJV)—CALLED THEM "SONS OF THE PROPHETS"

The sons of the prophets, that were at Bethel came forth to Elisha. Elisha advances from student to Master Prophet.

- Elisha revisits **GILGAL which means "Circle,"** according to Wikipedia. This is where he first started with Elijah. God sent him back so that he could be used in the time of famine. He turns 20 loaves of bread into more than enough to feed 100 people. The stew was poison, so he put meal in it and a miracle was performed. Having faith in God will cause miraculous things to happen. Read 2 Kings 4:38-44.

- There were three schools located in the communities of Bethel, Jericho, and Jordan River. These prophets were devoted to God and served God. They followed the teachings of Elijah, Elisha, and Samuel. The prophets were their students.

The Prophetic Flow Begins

Genesis 2:10-14 (KJV): "And a river went out of Eden to water the garden; and from there it was parted and became into four heads. The name of the first is **Pi'son**: that is, it which compasses the whole land of Hav'i-lah, where there is gold; And the gold of that land is good: there is bdellium and the onyx stone. And the name of the second river is **Gi'hon**: the same is that compasses the whole land of E-thi-o'pi-a. And the name of the third river is **Hid'de-kel**: that is, it which goes toward the east of As-syr'i-a. And the fourth river is **Eu-phra'tes."**

Prophetic is Flowing Rivers of God's Revelation

- **Eden**: God's original garden had four rivers flowing out of it. We are His garden today, and we communicate His Word and Revelation.
- **PISON**: gold, increase, full of flow, full of His presence.
- **GIHON:** bursting forth, overflow, and gushing. "But whosoever drinketh of the water that I shall give him, shall never thirst again, in him shall be a well springing up into everlasting Life." -John 4:14 (KJV).
- **HID-DE-KEL**: rapid, swift.
- **EUPHRATES**: fruitfulness, sweet.

"There is a river, the streams whereof shall make glad the city of God, the holy place of the tabernacles of the Most High. God is in the midst of her; she shall not be moved: God shall help her and that right early." -Psalm 46:4-5 (KJV).

The Office of a Prophet

- The Office of a Prophet holds a greater authority to speak and walk in a greater authority and power.
- 2 Kings 1:1-17 (KJV): This was not a prophecy of anger. The office of a prophet has greater command and demand.
- When God speaks, sometimes people want you to change what God is saying.
- Example of a word curse: when a person speaks from a place of anger. Because they are mad, this is a way of a word curse being released. "You reap what you sow." **(To be discussed more in the classroom setting.)**

The Gift of Prophecy

1 Corinthians 12:1-11 (KJV): "Now concerning the spiritual gifts, brethren, I would not have you ignorant. Ye know that ye were Gentiles, carried away unto these dumb idols, even as ye were led. Wherefore I give you to understand, that no man speaking by the Spirit of God calleth Jesus accursed: and that no man can say that Jesus is the Lord, but by the Holy Ghost. Now there are diversities of gifts, but the same Spirit. And there are differences of administrations, but the same Lord. And there are diversities of operations, but it is the same God which worketh all in all. But the manifestations of the Spirit is given to every man to profit withal. For to one is given by the Spirit the word of wisdom; to another the word of knowledge by the same Spirit; to another faith by the same Spirit; to another the gifts of healing by the same Spirit; to another the working of miracles; to another **Prophecy;** to another discerning of spirits, to another divers kinds of tongues; to another the interpretation of tongues. But all these worketh that one and the selfsame Spirit, dividing to every man severally as he will."

- Saul was anointed by Samuel to prophesy.

"And when they were come down from the high place into the city, Samuel communed with Saul upon the top of the house. And they arose early: and it came to pass about the spring of the day, that Samuel called Saul to the top of the house, saying, Up, that I may send the away. And Saul arose, and they went out the both of them, he and Samuel, abroad. And as they were going down to the end of the city, Samuel said to Saul, Bid the servant to pass on before us, (and he passed on), but stand thou still a while, that I may shew the word of God." – 1 Samuel 9:25-27 (KJV).

- Read 1 Samuel, Chapter 10. **(To be explained in the classroom setting.)**

Prophet in Training Series Preparation

- Week of training, students will be asked to fast from 6 a.m. – 6 p.m. Tuesday through Thursday.
- The fast should consist of liquids, fruits, and vegetables. If you are on medication, please consult with your doctor.
- During these hours of fasting, take some time to read, pray, and worship, and let the Holy Spirit lead you.
- This is to condition and shape you.
- Seek to yield to the Lord. Don't just seek to get a message. Yielding is submission.
- Prophecy is not your imagination.
- You will learn your way around; surroundings in the spirit realm to be able to speak what the Holy Spirit tells you.
- Where there's doubt, there will be less movement, less flow.
- Distractions prevent you from yielding.
- First and foremost, prophets are trained by our Lord Jesus Christ himself through the Holy Spirit.

LESSON ONE

ARE YOU CALLED TO BE A PROPHET?

Lesson Read-1 Kings 19:1-21 (KJV).

1 Kings 19:1-21: "And Ahab told Jezebel all that Elijah had done, and withal how he had slain all the prophets with the sword. Then Jezebel sent a messenger unto Elijah, saying, So let the gods do to me, and more also, if I make not thy life as the life of one of them by tomorrow about this time. And when he saw that, he arose, and went for his life, and came to Beersheba, which belongeth to Judah, and left his servant there. But he himself went a day's journey into the wilderness and came and sat down under a juniper tree: and he requested for himself that he might die; and said, It is enough; now, O Lord, take away my life; for I am not better than my fathers. And as he lay and slept under a juniper tree, behold, then an angel touched him, and said unto him, Arise and eat. And he looked, and, behold, there was a cake baken on the coals, and a cruse of water at his head. And he did eat and drink and laid him down again. And the angel of the Lord came again the second time, and touched him, and said, Arise and eat; because the journey is too great for thee. And he arose, and did eat and drink, and went in the strength of that meat forty days and forty nights unto Horeb the mount of God. And he came thither unto a cave, and lodged there; and, behold, the word of the Lord came to him, and he said unto him, What doest thou here, Elijah? And he said, I have been very jealous for the Lord God of hosts: for the children of Israel have forsaken thy covenant, thrown down thine altars, and slain thy prophets with the sword; and I, even I only, am left; and they seek my life, to take it away. And he said, Go forth, and stand upon the mount before the Lord. And, behold, the Lord passed by, and a great and strong wind rent the mountains, and brake in pieces the rocks before the Lord; but the Lord was not in the wind: and after the wind an earthquake; but the Lord was not in the earthquake: And after the earthquake a fire; but the Lord was not in the fire: and after the fire a still small voice. And it was so, when Elijah heard it, that he wrapped his face in his mantle, and went out, and stood in the entering in of the cave. And, behold, there came a voice unto him, and said, What doest thou here, Elijah? And he said, I have been very jealous for the Lord God of hosts: because the children of Israel have forsaken thy covenant, thrown down thine altars, and slain thy prophets with the sword; and I, even I only, am left; and they seek my

life, to take it away. And the Lord said unto him, Go, return on thy way to the wilderness of Damascus: and when thou comest, anoint Hazael to be king over Syria: And Jehu the son of Nimshi shalt thou anoint to be king over Israel: and Elisha the son of Shaphat of Abelmeholah shalt thou anoint to be prophet in thy room. And it shall come to pass, that him that escapeth the sword of Hazael shall Jehu slay: and him that escapeth from the sword of Jehu shall Elisha slay. Yet I have left me seven thousand in Israel, all the knees which have not bowed unto Baal, and every mouth which hath not kissed him. So, he departed thence, and found Elisha the son of Shaphat, who was plowing with twelve yoke of oxen before him, and he with the twelfth: and Elijah passed by him and cast his mantle upon him. And he left the oxen, and ran after Elijah, and said, Let me, I pray thee, kiss my father and my mother, and then I will follow thee. And he said unto him, Go back again: for what have I done to thee? And he returned back from him, and took a yoke of oxen, and slew them, and boiled their flesh with the instruments of the oxen, and gave unto the people, and they did eat. Then he arose, and went after Elijah, and ministered unto him."

- Elisha knew he was called to be a prophet because Elijah walked up to him and put his mantle around him and then he walked away.
- I am here to fan the flames, stir up the gifts, the office inside of you, to help you to the dimension as the Holy Spirit leads me to lead you.
- A mantle represents spiritual covering, cloak, release of gifting.
- John 14:12 talks about greater works.

How to Maintain the Flow of the Anointing

Lesson Read-2 Kings 4:1-7 (KJV).

2 Kings 4:1-7: "Now there cried a certain woman of the wives of the sons of the prophets unto Elisha, saying, Thy servant my husband is dead; and thou knowest that thy servant did fear the Lord: and the creditor is come to take unto him my two sons to be bondmen. And Elisha said unto her, What shall I do for thee? tell me, what hast thou in the house? And she said, Thine handmaid hath not anything in the house, save a pot of oil. Then he said, Go, borrow thee vessels abroad of all thy neighbours, even empty vessels; borrow not a few. And when thou art come in, thou shalt shut the door upon thee and upon thy sons, and shalt pour out into all those vessels, and thou shalt set aside that which is full. So, she went from him,

and shut the door upon her and upon her sons, who brought the vessels to her; and she poured out. And it came to pass, when the vessels were full, that she said unto her son, Bring me yet a vessel. And he said unto her, There is not a vessel more. And the oil stayed. Then she came and told the man of God. And he said, Go, sell the oil, and pay thy debt, and live thou and thy children of the rest."

Note: The oil will not run dry if you're open to receive a new anointing. Ask God for it. Ask Him for jars into which the oil can be poured (Who do I need to minister to, pour into spiritually and prophetically?)

Lesson for a Prophet

Elijah shared with us about keeping the anointing flowing. He gave the widow instructions to prevent the oil from running out.

1. **Examine your attitude.** The first order Elijah gave the widow had to do with maintaining a correct attitude. "Don't be afraid." The widow at Zarephath had to stop believing that she and her son were going to die. She had to free her mind of negative thoughts and disbelief. Elijah said to her, *"Fear not; go and do as you have said; but make me thereof a little cake first, and bring it to me, and after make for you and your son."* -1 Kings 17:13 (KJV).

2. **Establish your priorities.** Elijah addressed priorities when the woman told him her problem. Elijah's response was to go home and do as said. *"First, make a small cake of bread for me, from what you have and bring it to me, and then make for yourself and your son."*

3. **The word "first" is significant.** It seems as if Elijah was being insensitive. Although he knew this poor widow had little food, he asked her to provide for him first. But in doing so, Elijah was applying a basic principle for the widow to receive God's blessings.

4. **This principle applies to our finances, but it also applies to everything else**. Give to God first.

5. **Consecrate your life to God.** The Merriam-Webster's dictionary defines consecrate as "to declare to be sacred or holy."

6. **Be obedient**. Make sure you live a life of obedience. The Bible declares, "If ye be willing and obedient, ye shall eat the good of the land" -Isaiah 1:19 (KJV).

Time with God

Time with God is important. Prayer must be a daily practice for every believer. We must be alone with Him at times. **Seek** more of **Him** and we will see our anointing increase.

Sharing the Anointing

Elijah and Elisha had similar ministries. Elisha performed a miracle of provision for a widow.

Vessels to Fill

The people around you—at home, at work, in the neighborhood, in your school—are empty jars. They are needy, lacking all those things that only Jesus Christ can produce in our lives. *Then he said, "Go, borrow vessels abroad of all your neighbors, even empty vessels: borrow not a few."-* 2 Kings 4:2 (KJV).

<u>Prophecies of Rebuke</u>

Lesson Read-Ezekiel 16:15-16, 1 Kings 21:21-29, and 2 Kings 9:30-37 (KJV).

Ezekiel 16:15-16: "But thou didst trust in thine own beauty, and playedst the harlot because of thy renown, and pouredst out thy fornications on every one that passed by; his it was. And of thy garments thou didst take, and deckedst thy high places with divers colours, and playedst the harlot thereupon: the like things shall not come, neither shall it be so."

- These words indict (brings to trial). God's people are forgetting that their fame and fortune were God's gift and not their own doing. They relied on themselves and their gifts instead of God. They were becoming spiritually corrupt.

2 Kings 21:21-29: "Behold, I will bring evil upon thee, and will take away thy posterity, and will cut off from Ahab him that pisseth against the wall, and him that is shut up and left in Israel, And will make thine house like the house of Jeroboam

the son of Nebat, and like the house of Baasha the son of Ahijah, for the provocation wherewith thou hast provoked me to anger, and made Israel to sin. And of Jezebel also spake the Lord, saying, The dogs shall eat Jezebel by the wall of Jezreel. Him that dieth of Ahab in the city the dogs shall eat; and him that dieth in the field shall the fowls of the air eat. But there was none like unto Ahab, which did sell himself to work wickedness in the sight of the Lord, whom Jezebel his wife stirred up. And he did very abominably in following idols, according to all things as did the Amorites, whom the Lord cast out before the children of Israel. And it came to pass, when Ahab heard those words, that he rent his clothes, and put sackcloth upon his flesh, and fasted, and lay in sackcloth, and went softly. Seest thou how Ahab humbleth himself before me? because he humbleth himself before me, I will not bring the evil in his days: but in his son's days will I bring the evil upon his house."

- The curse was reversed on Jezebel's husband. Elijah prophesied to Jezebel and Ahab how they made Israel sin. Ahab feared the Lord and began to fast. And because he humbled himself and turned from evil, evil did not come upon him, but upon his sons.

2 Kings 9:30-37: "And when Jehu was come to Jezreel, Jezebel heard of it; and she painted her face, and tired her head, and looked out at a window. And as Jehu entered in at the gate, she said, Had Zimri peace, who slew his master? And he lifted up his face to the window, and said, Who is on my side? who? And there looked out to him two or three eunuchs. And he said, Throw her down. So, they threw her down: and some of her blood was sprinkled on the wall, and on the horses: and he trode her under foot. And when he was come in, he did eat and drink, and said, Go, see now this cursed woman, and bury her: for she is a king's daughter. And they went to bury her: but they found no more of her than the skull, and the feet, and the palms of her hands. Wherefore they came again and told him. And he said, This is the word of the Lord, which he spake by his servant Elijah the Tishbite, saying, In the portion of Jezreel shall dogs eat the flesh of Jezebel: And the carcase of Jezebel shall be as dung upon the face of the field in the portion of Jezreel; so that they shall not say, This is Jezebel."

- They found no more than the skull and the feet and the palms of her hands. This is the word of the Lord which was spoken by his servant Elijah the Tishbite. (refer to verses 35 and 36).

Divine Appointment

Lesson Read-2 Kings 2:1-8 (KJV).

2 Kings 2:1-18: "And it came to pass, when the Lord would take up Elijah into heaven by a whirlwind, that Elijah went with Elisha from Gilgal. And Elijah said unto Elisha, Tarry here, I pray thee; for the Lord hath sent me to Bethel. And Elisha said unto him, As the Lord liveth, and as thy soul liveth, I will not leave thee. So, they went down to Bethel. And the sons of the prophets that were at Bethel came forth to Elisha, and said unto him, Knowest thou that the Lord will take away thy master from thy head to day? And he said, Yea, I know it; hold ye your peace. And Elijah said unto him, Elisha, tarry here, I pray thee; for the Lord hath sent me to Jericho. And he said, As the Lord liveth, and as thy soul liveth, I will not leave thee. So, they came to Jericho. And the sons of the prophets that were at Jericho came to Elisha, and said unto him, Knowest thou that the Lord will take away thy master from thy head to day? And he answered, Yea, I know it; hold ye your peace. And Elijah said unto him, Tarry, I pray thee, here; for the Lord hath sent me to Jordan. And he said, As the Lord liveth, and as thy soul liveth, I will not leave thee. And they two went on. And fifty men of the sons of the prophets went and stood to view afar off: and they two stood by Jordan. And Elijah took his mantle, and wrapped it together, and smote the waters, and they were divided hither and thither, so that they two went over on dry ground."

- Divine: of God, directly from God, or like God.
    - The Lord made it clear to Elijah that his time was at hand. He therefore went to the different School of the Prophets to give them his last exhortation and blessings.
    - The divine appointment was two-fold: Elijah would be taken into heaven by a whirlwind and Elisha would receive a double portion.
    - The revelation of Elijah's dying appointment was revealed to the prophets and to Elisha. The prophets tried to reveal it, but Elisha told them to keep silent because he was to receive the *mantle*, *mandate*, and the *mission* so his assignment would be completed.

How Bad Do You Want It?

Lesson Read-Philippians 3:6-10 (KJV).

Philippians 3:6-10: "Concerning zeal, persecuting the church; touching the righteousness which is in the law, blameless. But what things were gain to me, those I counted loss for Christ. Yea doubtless, and I count all things but loss for the excellency of the knowledge of Christ Jesus my Lord: for whom I have suffered the loss of all things, and do count them but dung, that I may win Christ, And be found in him, not having mine own righteousness, which is of the law, but that which is through the faith of Christ, the righteousness which is of God by faith: that I may know him, and the power of his resurrection, and the fellowship of his sufferings, being made conformable unto his death."

Gilgal: separation from the flesh, the past. -Philippians 3:6-7 (KJV).

Bethel: house of God, desire to know God and to be in His presence. -Philippians 3:8 (KJV).

Jericho: faith walk. -Philippians 3:9 (KJV).

Jordan: death and resurrection. -Philippians 3:10 (KJV).

Gilgal: circle, stone, hard place.

Bethel: place of worship.

Jericho: completion, wholeness in the prophetic office.

Jordan: crossing over, set-apart to receive the double portion.

Samuel Anoints Saul to Prophecy

Lesson Read-1 Samuel 9:27 and 10: 1-13 (KJV).

1 Samuel 9:27: "And as they were going down to the end of the city, Samuel said to Saul, bid the servant pass on before us, (and he passed on), but stand thou still a while that I may shew thee the word of God."

1 Samuel 10:1-13: "Then Samuel took a vial of oil, and poured it upon his head, and kissed him, and said, Is it not because the Lord hath anointed thee to be captain

over his inheritance? When thou art departed from me today, then thou shalt find two men by Rachel's sepulchre in the border of Benjamin at Zelzah; and they will say unto thee, The asses which thou wentest to seek are found: and, lo, thy father hath left the care of the asses, and sorroweth for you, saying, What shall I do for my son? Then shalt thou go on forward from thence, and thou shalt come to the plain of Tabor, and there shall meet thee three men going up to God to Bethel, one carrying three kids, and another carrying three loaves of bread, and another carrying a bottle of wine: And they will salute thee band give thee two loaves of bread; which thou shalt receive of their hands. After that thou shalt come to the hill of God, where is the garrison of the Philistines: and it shall come to pass, when thou art come thither to the city, that thou shalt meet a company of prophets coming down from the high place with a psaltery, and a tabret, and a pipe, and a harp, before them; and they shall prophesy: And the Spirit of the Lord will come upon thee, and thou shalt prophesy with them, and shalt be turned into another man. And let it be, when these signs are come unto thee, that thou do as occasion serve thee; for God is with thee. And thou shalt go down before me to Gilgal; and, behold, I will come down unto thee, to offer burnt offerings, and to sacrifice sacrifices of peace offerings: seven days shalt thou tarry, till I come to thee, and shew thee what thou shalt do. And it was so, that when he had turned his back to go from Samuel, God gave him another heart: and all those signs came to pass that day. And when they came thither to the hill, behold, a company of prophets met him; and the Spirit of God came upon him, and he prophesied among them. And it came to pass, when all that knew him beforetime saw that, behold, he prophesied among the prophets, then the people said one to another, What is this that is come unto the son of Kish? Is Saul also among the prophets? And one of the same place answered and said, But who is their father? Therefore, it became a proverb, Is Saul also among the prophets? And when he had made an end of prophesying, he came to the high place."

- The anointing of a ruler was a religious act, which is why David had such high regard for Saul, refusing to lift a hand against the "Lords anointed."
- The inheritance—the land of Israel—was God's gift to his people, but it would return to God's direct control if the people did not manage it according to God's law.
- Giving bread to Saul was a sacred act, as well as a sign for Saul.
- God's Spirit prepared Saul for kingship.
- The Spirit of the Lord would come upon them on the Old Testament at certain times for them to accomplish their assignments or tasks.

- Saul wanted to worship God, but he continually struggled with wanting to do things his way.
- The vial of oil was the holy oil which the priest was anointed, throughout the Holy Scriptures. Ceremony of investiture with royal office among the Hebrews was done because this was an impartation for an assignment, office, or priestly authority.
- Samuel represented the authority and power of God. He kissed Saul and gave him a symbol and token.
- Samuel quiets Saul's doubt and gave him three signs to convince him that his appointment was from God: (1) thou shall find two men by Rachel's sepulcher, (2) you will meet three men going up to God to Bethel, and (3) you shall meet a company of prophets.

NOTES

LESSON TWO
CHARACTER

Lesson Read-1 Corinthians 14:3 (KJV).

1 Corinthians 14:3: "But he that prophesieth speaketh unto men to *edification*, and *exhortation*, and *comfort*."

Edification: "The instruction or improvement of the person." This is the building of the soul, a spiritual improvement. This is a process of edifying.

Exhortation: "Encouragement, urging someone to do something." Paul said in many letters "I exhort you." To console a person or to also rebuke, it's still encouraging when you're being corrected.

Comfort: ("Parakleo" Greek), means Comforter. You can't have true comfort without the Comforter.

- What comes with comfort? Deposits, to make free, establishing, casting down something that shouldn't be in one's life.

Godly Character: According to one source, godly character is defined as "Having the ability to discern God's right way from the wrong, you voluntarily surrender your will to what's right in God's eyes." God wants us to be authentic. When character is exercised *faith* is exercised.

Character: "Personality, nature, temperament of an individual."

- A prophet is God's spokesperson, a mouthpiece on earth. Speaking for God is impossible unless some of the *Character of God* is manifested. *Godly character* is essential.
- God is concerned with the messenger. The minister is more important than the ministry of what you are called to do. If the minister is wrong, the message will be wrong. Protect and preserve your reputation.

Keys That are Present in a Prophet

Demonstration of the Spirit and of the Power of God.

1 Corinthians 2:4-5 (KJV): "And my speech and my preaching was not with enticing words of man's wisdom, but in demonstration of the Spirit and of power: That your faith should not stand in the wisdom of men, but in the power of God."

1. **Power of the Spirit**

Prophets must be full of Power of the Holy Spirit. Without the Holy Spirit, a prophet can't function. As we read the scriptures, it is with clear understanding that the prophets must have the Spirit of God and demonstration of His power and authority. True prophets have absolutely no power in and of themselves. All that is accomplished must be by the Holy Spirit. Prophets are trained by the Holy Spirit, the master teacher of all. Prophets should walk in the Spirit, praying constantly. This means silent prayers as well as praying in tongues.

- "By your Spirit you warned them through your prophets."- Nehemiah 9:30 (NIV).
- "I wish that all the Lord's people were prophets and that the Lord would put his spirit on them." -Numbers 11:29 (NIV).
- "I will pour out my Spirit on all people your sons and your daughter will prophesy." Acts 2:17 (NIV).
- "His father Zechariah was filled with the Holy Spirit and prophesied." - Luke 1:67 (NIV).

2. **Total Obedience**
- A prophet must be totally obedient to God.
- The prophetic holds a high standard.
- 1 Kings, Chapter 13 tells of a young prophet who started well but ended in disaster because of failing to obey what God had spoken to him. Prophets be reminded of this chapter. It will help you understand how important it is to be obedient to God. This chapter shows us a *Disobedient Prophet*.
- Balaam did not practice what he preached, but was clear about obedience to God. "And Balaam said unto Ba'-lak Lo, I am come unto thee: have I

now any power at all to say anything? The word that God putteth in my mouth, that shall I speak." Numbers 22:38 (KJV).

- Elisha obeyed. He forsook being a farmer and became an adjutant for Elijah. He learned obedience. He served the anointing. -1 Kings 19:21 (KJV).
- Armour bearer is one who serves. It is an honor and privilege to hold this position. It expresses servitude, serving the Lord and the leader.

3. **Peace with God**
   - Prophets must be at peace with God.
   - Prophets will get it wrong. The solution to correcting it is to repent and turn back to God.
   - God promised Jeremiah protection. He had a repentant attitude.-Jeremiah 15:19-21 (KJV).
   - Prophetic ministries require deep communion with God, making your relationship with Him important.

4. **Patience**
   - Waiting is very important in the prophetic ministry. You will spend much time waiting on God. This is part of conditioning and discipline so that you will continue to rely on Him and the Holy Spirit. -Daniel 12:9 (KJV).

5. **Integrity and honesty**
   - The first loyalty of a prophet is the truth. To have credibility, truth, and integrity are the life of a prophet.
   - Elijah was true to the call when he dealt with issues of truth. For the glory to be restored in the church and the spirit of God to be restored, you have to be truthful to all.

6. **Humility**
   - Pride kills prophets. The greatest threat to the prophetic ministry is pride. Your life will be established with a deep work of humility when you are intended to speak for Him. Humility is much needed.
   - The church at Corinth was reminded the most mature prophet doesn't have all the knowledge. -1 Corinthians 13:8-10 (KJV).

7. **Compassion**
   - In the Old Testament the prophets were uncompromising, and they shed more tears because compassion was at the heart of their ministries. God is *love* so His truth must be spoken in *love*. When the message is harder, it is important that it is spoken with compassion. Jeremiah had to deal with the word the Lord spoke to him to speak to the people. -Jeremiah 8:21 and 9:1 (KJV).

8. **Commitment and Tenacity**
   - Be firm, determined, persistent.
   - Prophets will meet opposition.
   - Opposition comes from the people who know you well. -Jeremiah. 12:5-6 (KJV).
   - John 4:44 (KJV) tells us that *"a prophet has no honor in his own country."*
   - Prophets must meet opposition with an attitude of tenacity and be committed totally to their ministry as a prophet.

9. **Boldness and courage**
   - Loyalty to God sometimes puts us in dangerous positions of opposition. Ezekiel 3:4-10 (KJV).
   - To fulfill the prophetic ministry, it requires boldness to speak what God says and to face head on the situation spiritually.

10. **Preparation**
    - There is a price paid for *character*. Years are spent for preparation.
    - Look at the lives of Isaiah, Ezekiel, Jeremiah, and many more of God's anointed.
    - Preparing through fasting is discipline. Praying is communication with God. Reading the Word of God and getting to know Him through Revelation of the Word is very important.

Prophetic Activation Exercises

- Eli taught Samuel how to discern, respond and become sensitive to the voice of God.

- Prophets can only teach you how to cooperate with the activity of the Holy Spirit, not how to manufacture the Holy Spirit activity. The Holy Spirit cannot be *fabricated*.
- It is important to spend quality time in the presence of God and understand your responsibility to minister to God, and then to His people.
- Worship is the doorway to receiving a revelation from God.
- Arouse your dormancy; stir up the gifts in you.
- Matthew 7:7 (KJV) says, "Ask, seek, and knock," and Jeremiah 33:3 (KJV) says, "I will answer thee and shew thee *great* and *mighty* things." Secrets, mysteries, inaccessible things.
- Bringing light to chaos means bringing life and order.
- Focus. Look in the Spirit. What do I see, feel, or have a knowing about the situation? God speaks through your spirit. -Isaiah 21:3-4 (KJV).
- Manifestation means to see and behold.
- The end result of prophecy is to find a way to put honor and glory back on mankind and restore what we lost in the garden: relationship to the Father. -Psalm 8:4-5 (KJV).
- Prophecy releases the Power of God. -1 Samuel 2:35 (KJV).
- Recognize His thoughts. -1 Corinthians 2:16 (KJV).
- "It is the spirit that quickeneth; the flesh profiteth nothing: the words that I speak unto you, they are spirit, and they are life." -John 6:63 (KJV).

NOTES

LESSON THREE

GROWING IN THE PROPHETIC

There are different levels of gifting and authority. There are major prophets and minor prophets. Jesus had three in His inner circle that He could take to the mountain with Him for the transfiguration. I am led to believe that there was a transfer for these three apostles. You want to have leadership with a "prophetic edge," meaning you will have prophetic teachings and preaching. The surface of your ministry in leadership should have prophetic gifting, character, prophetic words, and that does not always mean there is an office of a prophet. Prophets are not the only persons able to experience the prophetic. We all have the gift of prophecies; the Holy Ghost inside of us is the *gift*. The prophetic is a divine move of God's spirit.

Functioning of the Prophetic

The Ear of Understanding is more than your physical ear. Your spirit man perceives the voice and receives the voice beyond the physical ear.

Lesson read- 1 Sam. 3:1-8 (KJV).

The Seeing Eye is vision which allows one to see in the realm of the spirit, beyond physical capabilities. It is function that precedes our ability.

- "In the year that King Uz-zi'ah died I saw also the Lord sitting upon a throne high and lifted up, and His train filled the temple." – Isaiah 6:1 (KJV). This is an elevated place Isaiah was in.

The Voice of the Anointing affects one's situation, circumstance, or accomplishments.

- "So shall My word be that goes forth out of My mouth: it shall not return to Me void, but it shall accomplish that which I please, and it shall prosper in the thing whereto I sent it." – Isaiah- 55:11 (KJV).

- "Now in the morning as He returned into the city, He hungered. And when He saw the fig tree in the way, He came to it, and found nothing thereon, but leaves only, and said to it, Let no fruit grow on you from now on forever. And presently the fig tree withered away." – Matthew 21:18-19 (KJV).

The Walk of Manifestation is realized as the spirit man that is "dominant" or the "prevailing man," speaking with authority.

- "And there sat a certain man at Lys'stra, impotent in his feet, being a cripple from his mother's womb, who never walked: the same heard Peter speak: who steadfastly beholding him, and perceiving that he had faith to be healed, said with a loud voice, Stand upright on your feet. And he leaped and walked." – Acts 14:8-10 (KJV).
- He who prophecies speaks edification, and exhortation, and comfort to men.
- There's increase in the prophetic revelation, and there's an outpouring.
  - "And it shall come to pass in the last days, says God, I will pour out of My Spirit upon all flesh: and your sons and your daughters shall prophesy, and your young men shall see visions, and your old men shall dream dreams. And on My servants and on My handmaidens, I will pour out in those days of My spirit; and they shall prophesy." - Acts 2:17-18 (KJV).
- You cannot do anything without the Holy Spirit.
  - "And He gave some, apostles; and some, prophets; and some, evangelists; and some, pastors and teachers; for the perfecting of the saints, for the work of the ministry, for the edifying of the body of Christ." - Ephesians 4:11-12 (KJV).

Covet the Ability to Prophecy.

- "Follow after charity, and desire spiritual gifts, but rather that you may prophesy." -1 Corinthians 14:1 (KJV).
- "Wherefore, brethren, covet to prophesy, and forbid not to speak with tongues." -1 Corinthians 14:39 (KJV).

The Spirit of Prophecy.

- "And I fell at his feet to worship him. And he said to me, see you do it not: I am your fellow-servant, and of your brethren that have the testimony of

Jesus: worship God: for the testimony of Jesus is the spirit of prophecy." - Revelation 19:10 (KJV).

- Old Testament anointing says, "Came upon"—revelation received.
- New Testament anointing says, "Came from within"—revelation perceived.

Training and Maturation Process

1 Samuel 1: 24-28 (KJV): "And when she had weaned him, she took him up with her, with three bullocks, and one ephah of flour, and a bottle of wine, and brought him to the house of the Lord in Shi'loh: and the child was young. And they slew the bullock and brought the child to E'li. And she said, Oh my lord, as your soul lives, my lord, I am the woman that stood by you here, praying to the Lord. For this child I prayed: and the Lord has given me my petition which I asked of Him: Therefore, also I have lent him to the Lord; as long as he lives shall he be lent to the Lord. And he worshipped the Lord there."

- Hannah was barren. She made a vow to the Lord that if He would give her a son, she would give him back to the Lord.
- This symbolizes an intimate relationship with God, because she sought God, but also made a vow.
- She was willing to surrender. Are you willing to surrender all to God and to give all that is inside of you, your heart?

Training Under Spiritual Supervision

- The word "minister" means to attend, serve, wait. Part of what it means to be a prophet is learning to SERVE in ministry.
- The word "before" means under supervision of. The budding prophet must serve the Lord under the supervision of an apostle, prophet, or pastor in a local church.
- Are the budding prophets willing to serve in any capacity if asked in order to show their labor of love?
- It is important for a growing prophet to be fathered in a ministry.
  - "So he departed from there, and found E-li'sha the son Sha'phat, who was plowing with twelve yoke of oxen before him, and with the twelfth: and E-li'jah passed by him, and cast his mantle upon. And he left the oxen, and ran after E-li'jah, and said, Let me I prau you, kiss my father, and my mother, and then I will follow you. And he said to

him, Go back again: for what have I done to you? And he returned back from him, and took, a yoke of oxen, and slew them, and boiled their flesh with the instruments of the oxen, and gave to the people, and they did eat. The he arose, and went after E-li'jah, and ministered to him." -1 Kings 19:19-21 (KJV).

- Dedication is important in the training process. You will need to be dedicated in order to be taught the spiritual things of the prophetic ministry, and character development.

Prophets Must Be Fathered by an Experienced Prophet

- Paul trained Timothy and expected Timothy to do the same with those under his leadership.
- Paul never took possession or claimed ownership over Timothy's life: he had stewardship that involved him nurturing him spiritually.
- No one has the right to control someone; it is OUT OF ORDER.

Speaking Through Impartation

The Word of God gives us different kinds of impartations. **Impartation** derived from Greek, meaning metadidomi (met-ad-id'-o-mee): to give over, share, imparticle.

- "For I long to see you, that I may impart to you some spiritual gift, so that you be established that is, that I may be encouraged together with you by the mutual faith both of you and me." – Romans 1:11-12 (NKJV).

Impartation Through Laying on of Hands

Laying on of hands in the Old Testament was an act of blessing.

- "And Israel stretched out his right hand, and laid it upon Ephraim's head, who was the younger, and his left hand upon Manasseh's head, guiding his hands wittingly; for Ma-nas'seh was the firstborn. And he blessed Joseph, and said, God, before whom my fathers, Abraham and Isaac did walk, the God which fed me all my life long to this day." – Genesis 48:14-15 (KJV).
- "And you shall cause a bullock to be brought before the tabernacle of the congregation: and Aaron and his sons shall put their hands upon the head of

the bullock. And you shall kill the bullock before the Lord by the door of the tabernacle of the congregation." – Exodus 29:10-11 (KJV).

- "And when had made an end of reconciling the holy place, and the tabernacle of the congregation, and the altar, he shall bring the live goat: And Aaron shall lay both his hands upon the head of the live goat, and confess over him all the iniquities of the children Israel and all their transgressions in all their sins, putting them upon the head of the goat, and shall send him away by the hand of a fit man into the wilderness." – Leviticus 16:20-21 (KJV).
- "And you shall bring the Levites before the Lord: and the children of Israel shall put their hands upon the Levites: And Aaron shall offer the Levites before the Lord for an offering of the children of Israel, that they may execute the service of the Lord." – Numbers 8:10-11 (KJV).

Laying on of hands in the New Testament was an act to receive the Holy Spirit

- "Who, when they were come down, prayed for them, that they might receive the Holy Ghost: For as yet He was fallen upon none of them: only they were baptized in the name of the Lord Jesus. They laid they their hands on them, and they received the Holy Ghost". -Acts 8: 15-18 (KJV).
- "And when Paul had laid his hands upon them, the Holy Ghost came on them; and they spoke with tongues and prophesied." – Acts 19:6 (KJV).
- "Wherefore I put you in remembrance that you stir up the gift of God, which is in you by the putting on of my hands." – 1 Timothy 1:6 (KJV).
- "And they ministered to the Lord, and fasted, the Holy Ghost said, Separate Me Barnabas and Saul for the work of the whereto I have called them. And when they had fasted and prayed, and laid their hands on them, they sent them away." – Acts 13:2-3 (KJV).
- "They shall take up serpents; and if they drink any deadly thing, it shall not hurt them; they shall lay hands on the sick, and they shall recover." –Mark 16:18 (KJV).

Anointing is Transferred Through Touching

- "A lady pursued Jesus and received Jesus' virtue to heal her. He did not choose to give this to her, her faith went after Jesus and her need "drew" it out of Him. *Jesus said, "Somebody hath touched me."* Luke 8:46 (KJV).

Anointing is Transferred Through a Corporate Impartation

- In the Old Testament, Saul mingled with the prophets. He received the same spirit of prophecy: "And the spirit of the Lord will come upon you, and you shall prophesy with them, and shall be turned into another man". –1 Samuel 10:6 (KJV).

Anointing is Transferred Through Distance

The anointing can be transferred through distance by speaking the Word. You could be watching an online service, TV, etc. There's a release in it.

- "The centurion answered and said, Lord, I am not worthy that You should come under my roof: **but speak the word only, and my servant shall be healed**. For I am a man under authority, having soldiers under me: and I say to this man Go, and he goes: and to another, Come, and he comes; and to my servant, Do this, and he does it. When Jesus heard it, He marveled, and said to them that followed, Verily I say to you, I have not found so great faith, no, not in Israel". – Matthew 8:8-10 (KJV).

Anointing Is Transferred Straight From Heaven: An Outpouring

- "And suddenly there came a sound from heaven as of a rushing mighty wind, and it filled all the house where they were sitting. And there appeared to them cloven tongues like as of fire, and it sat upon each of them. And they were all filled with the Holy Ghost, and began to speak with other tongues, and the Spirit gave them utterance." – Acts 2:2-4 (KJV).

Impartation of the Anointing Through Anointing Oil

Oil that has been set aside and consecrated unto the Lord for His purposes can be used to impart His anointing.

- "And you shall make it an oil of holy ointment, and ointment compound after the art of the apothecary: it shall be a holy anointing oil. And you shall anoint the tabernacle of the congregation therewith, and ark of the testimony. And the table and all its vessels, and the candlesticks and its vessels, and the altar of the incense, and the altar of burned offering with all its vessels, and the laver and its foot. And you shall sanctify them, that they may be most holy; whatsoever touches them shall be holy. And you shall anoint Aaron and his sons, and consecrate them, that they may minister to Me in the priest's office." – Exodus 30:25-30 (KJV).
- "And it shall come to pass in that day, that his burden shall be taken away from off your shoulder, and his yoke from off your neck, and the yoke shall be destroyed because of the anointing." – Isaiah 10:27 (KJV).
- "Is any sick among you? Let him call for the elders of the church; and let them pray over him, anointing him with oil in the name of the Lord." – James 5:14 (KJV).

Anointing Imparted Through Anointed Belongings of Servants of God

- **Jesus' clothes:** "And besought Him that they might only touch the hem of His garment: and as many as touched were made perfectly whole." – Matthew 14:36 (KJV).
- **Elijah's mantle:** "And he took the mantle of Elijah that fell from him, and smote the waters, and said, where is the Lord God of Elijah? And when he also had smitten the waters, they parted here and there: and Elisha went over." – 2 Kings 2:14 (KJV).
- **Moses' rod:** "And the Lord said to Moses, "Go on before the people, and take with you of the elders of Israel; and your rod, wherewith you smote the river, take in your hand, and go. Behold, I will stand before you there upon the rock in Horeb; and you shall smite the rock, and there come water out of it, that the people may drink." And Moses did so in the sight of the elders of Israel." – Exodus 17:5-6 (KJV).

- **Handkerchiefs and Aprons:** "And God wrought special miracles by the hands of Paul: so that from his body were brought to the sick handkerchiefs or aprons, and the disease departed from them, and the evil spirits went out of them."– Acts 19:11-12 (KJV).

- **Elisha's Staff:** Then he said to Gehazi, Gird up your loins, and take my staff in your hand, and go your way: if you meet any man, salute him not; and if any salute you, answer him not again: and lay my staff upon the face of the child. -2 Kings 4:29 (KJV).

- **Peter's Shadow:** "Insomuch that they brought forth the sick into the streets, and laid them on beds and couches, that at the least the shadow of Peter passing by might overshadow some of them". -Acts 5:15 (KJV).

- **Elisha's bones:** "And it came to pass, as they were burying a man, that, behold, they spied and band of men; and they cast the man into the sepulcher of Elisha: and when the man was let down, and touched the bones of Elisha, he revived, and stood upon his feet." -2 Kings 13:21(KJV).

NOTES

LESSON FOUR

THE FIVEFOLD MINISTRY

Lesson Read-Ephesians 4:11-13 (KJV).

Ephesians 4:11-13: "And He gave some apostles; and some, prophets; and some, evangelist; and some, pastors and teachers; For the perfecting of the saints, for the work of the ministry, for the work of the ministry, for the edifying of the body of Christ: Till we all come in the unity of the faith, and of the knowledge of the Son of God, to a perfect man, to the measure of the stature of the fullness of Christ

This is a study on how the local church should be governed, incorporating the ministry gifts of the apostles, prophets, evangelists, pastors, and teachers. This study is to develop an understanding of God's anointing and gifts.

- "With all thy getting get **understanding**." -Proverbs 4:7 (KJV).
- "How good and pleasant it is for brethren to dwell together in **UNITY.**" -Psalm 133 (KJV).
- In this study we will develop an understanding how the ministries should function together.
- There is an acronym that I use, SIYL, which means to "Stay In Your Lane," but yet walk in agreement.

The fivefold ministry is given by Jesus Christ to the church for the purpose of equipping the saints for the work of the ministry, building the Body of Christ.

- The fivefold is designed to minister to the church.
- The fivefold ministry can be misunderstood due to lack of understanding.
- Every believer of the fivefold ministry is to be held accountable to fulfill these gifts and mandates.
- We will study each ministry individually.

APOSTLE

The Greek word apostolos (ap-os'-tol-os) is translated to "apostle," meaning a delegate, an ambassador of the gospel; official, a commissioner of Jesus Christ; or one that is sent.

- An apostle represents the one from whom he received his commission. There appear to be more apostles of organizations than apostles of Jesus Christ.
- Apostles represents Jesus and the Kingdom of God to the people.
- An apostle is a person with the supernatural ability to give direction, set order, and to structure the church according to JESUS, who is the head of the church.
- In the Book of Acts, Peter and Paul were the first to start the apostolic ministry after the ascension of Jesus. As we read further in the New Testament, Paul gives a deeper insight into the apostolic ministry.
- The foundation of how we should build through the Body of Christ:
  - "And are built upon the foundation of the apostles and prophets, Jesus Christ Himself being the chief corner stone; in whom all the building fitly framed together grows to a holy temple in the Lord." -Ephesians 2:20-21 (KJV).
  - "According to the grace of God which is given to me, as a wise master builder, I have laid the foundation, and another builds thereon. But let every man take heed how he builds thereupon." – 1 Corinthians 3:10- (KJV).

PROPHET

The Greek word prophetes (pro-ay'-tace) is translated to "prophet," meaning a foreteller.

- The ministry gift of the prophet is a person with the supernatural ability to warn, correct, point to a direction, see visions, foretell, and interpret dreams through revelation of the Holy Spirit.
- Prophecy must edify, exhort, and comfort, NOT DESTROY.
- "Exhort" means to strongly encourage, charge a person to something.

- "Exhort "means in the Greek language to relieve in affliction, or to console a person.
- "Edification" means moral or spiritual instruction
- "Edification" in the Greek language, means to BUILD UP.
- "Comfort" means to relieve from worry or distress.
- "Comfort" in the Greek language means consolation.

EVANGELIST

The Greek word euaggelistes (yoo-ang-ghel-is-tace') translates to "evangelist," meaning a preacher of the gospel.

- An evangelist is a person with the supernatural ability to spread the gospel of Jesus Christ that people respond through repentance. Evangelists are soul winners for Christ to help build the Body of Christ. If an evangelist come in contact with a person that does not have a church home, they should encourage them to be a part of the ministry that they are a member of. They are NOT to open a church for themselves.
  - "And the next day we that were of Paul's company departed and came to Caesarea: and we entered into the house of Philip the evangelist, which was one of the seven; and abode with him." – Acts 21:8 (KJV).
- The evangelist is part of the birthing process, a midwife. This can be male or female. When we go to the doctor, we see male or female obstetricians.
- The evangelist is NOT a pastor or a teacher. He or she is a proclaimer of the gospel and of the Kingdom of God.

PASTOR

The Greek word poimen (poy-mane') is translated to "pastors and shepherd," meaning shepherd.

- The pastor is a person with the supernatural ability to lead, to feed, and to protect the flock. He or she is to lead by the Word of God, and they also lead by example. Pastors nourishes and develops the flock.
- In the Old Testament, pastors were identified as kings.
- In the New Testament, pastors were identified as shepherds.
- Pastors are responsible for the growth and health of the flock. This gift is gentler than the apostle and the prophet.

TEACHER

The Greek word didaskalos (did-as'-kal-os) is translated to "teacher," meaning instructor.

- The teacher is a person with the supernatural ability to explain clearly and effectively the truth of the Word of God.
- It's not an educational skill; this is a gift that requires time to explain detail.
- A teacher must exercise patience.

ORDER OF THE FIVEFOLD MINISTRY

- 1 Corinthians 12:28, Ephesians 2:20, Ephesians 4:11.
- The apostle sets the order of course.
- The prophet exhorts the people to get in order.
- The evangelist leads the people to order.
- The teacher instructs people to maturity.

It is important that the gift of the fivefold ministry work in order with each other so that it does not cause confusion. Most of the local churches don't have the proper foundation, such as the apostle and the prophet, to build the correct foundation.

UNDERSTANDING THE FUNCTION OF THE FIVEFOLD MINISTRY

Apostles

The apostles are the thumbs because this position touches all other parts of the fivefold ministry. A lot of people disagree and argue over this because they say all positions come in contact with the other. This is true, but it is the apostles that builds and fortify others in the remaining positions. If anything, the apostles are edifying to the congregation because their whole purpose is to build the ministers so strong that he or she can leave the church knowing there will still remain a function among the members of the Body of Christ. Lesson Read. Acts, Chapter 11 (KJV).

Prophets

The prophets are the index finger, but not because they are pointing out blunders. Prophets are meant to show the way (point you in the right direction), and to encourage others through the prophetic word. No prophetic word that is truly given by God will ever tear a person down and make them feel worse than they felt before hearing God's Word. Individual prophecy is meant to give direction and encouragement to the individual. Lesson Read. Acts, Chapter 21 (KJV).

Evangelists

The evangelists are the middle finger because it reaches outside the hand (the church body) before any other member. Evangelists are in so many different places in the community. Evangelists come in different forms that we may not even realize. Some of them are writers, artists, speakers, dancers, educators, officers, and sometimes politicians. They are integrated in the community. They evangelize to people and bring them into the church body, before the church body reaches the people.

Pastors

Pastors are the ring finger because they are married to God in the agreement that they lead the church as a man would be the spiritual leader in his home. The pastor is ultimately responsible for what happens in the church.

Teachers

Teachers are the pinky finger, and it is not because they are the smallest. Try tying your pinky finger down and go around using your hand. You will recognize that you just cannot do things as smoothly. Your movement will be unfocused. Teachers reveal the tiniest, most interesting details of scripture, things you would not have noticed or understood otherwise. Teachers are responsible for enhancing the love of God's Word in your mind.

NOTES

MORNING DEVOTIONAL

O GOD, you are my God; early will I seek You: my soul thirsts for You, my flesh longs for You in a dry and thirsty land, where no water is;

To see Your power and Your glory, so as I have seen you in the sanctuary.

Because Your lovingkindness is better than life, my lips shall praise you.

Thus will I bless You while I live: I will lift up my hands in Your name.

My soul shall be satisfied as with marrow and fatness; and my mouth shall praise You with joyful lips:

When I remember You upon my bed and meditate on You in the night watches.

Because You have been my help, therefore in the shadow of Your wings will I rejoice.

My soul follows hard after You: Your right hand upholds me.

But those that seek my soul, to destroy it, shall go into the lower parts of the earth.

They shall fall by the sword: they shall be a portion for foxes.

But the king shall rejoice in God; everyone that swears by Him shall glory: but the mouth them that speak lies shall be stopped.

Psalm 63 (KJV).

EVENING PRAYER

Lord, I cry to You: make haste to me; give ear to my voice, when I cry to You.

Let my prayer be set forth before You as incense; and the lifting up of my hands as the evening sacrifice.

Set a watch, O LORD, before my mouth; keep the door of my lips.

Incline not my heart to any evil thing, to practice wicked works with men that work iniquity: and let me not eat of their dainties.

Let the righteous smite me; it shall be a kindness: and let him reprove me; it shall be an excellent oil, which shall not break my head: for yet my prayer also shall be in their calamities.

When their judges are overthrown in stony places, they shall hear my words; for they are sweet.

Our bones are scattered at the grave's mouth, s when one cuts and splits wood upon the earth.

But my eyes are to you, O God the Lord: in You is my trust; leave not my soul destitute.

Keep me from the snares which they have laid for me, and the gins of the workers of iniquity.

Let the wicked fall into their own nets, until I with escape.

Psalm 141 (KJV).

PRAYER OF SURRENDER

I AM the true vine, and My Father is the husbandman.

Every branch in Me that bears not fruit He takes away: and every branch that bears fruit, He purges it, that it may bring forth more fruit.

Now you are clean through the word which I have spoken to you.

Abide in Me, and I in you. As the branch cannot bear fruit of itself, except it abide in the vine; no more can you, except you abide in Me.

I am the vine, you are the branches: He that abides in Me, and I in him, the same brings forth much fruit: for without Me you can do nothing.

If a man abide not in Me, he is cast forth as a branch, and is withered; and men gather them, and cast them into the fire, and they are burned.

If you abide in Me, and My words abide in you, you shall ask what you will, and it shall be done to you.

John 15:1-7 (KJV).

NAMES AND ATTRIBUTES OF GOD

- EL: The Strong One. Attributes- Almighty God, Everlasting God, The Living God, A Faithful God.
- ELOHIM: The Almighty.
- JEHOVAH: "He Is," The Self-Existing One.
- ADONAHY: Lord, Master.
- JEHOVAH NISSI: 'The Lord is my banner." Exodus.17:15 and Hebrews 12:2 (KJV).
- JEHOVAH ROPHI: "The Lord Who Heals You." Exodus 15:26 and John 9:1-7 (KJV).
- JEHOVAH JIREH: "The Lord Who Provides." Genesis 22:14 and Matthew 6:33 (KJV).
- JEHOVAH TSIDIKENU: "The Lord Our Righteousness." Jeremiah 23:6 and Romans 4:6,24 (KJV).
- JEHOVAH ROHI: "The Lord My Shepherd." Psalm 23:1 and John 10:14-15 (KJV).
- EL CHAI: "The Living God." Deuteronomy 5:25 and Revelation 1:18 (KJV).
- EL KANNA: "The Jealous God." Exodus 20:5 and John 2:13-17 (KJV).
- EL HANNUN: "The Merciful God." Deuteronomy 4:31 and John 8:10,11(KJV).
- EL AVRAHAM YITZAK: "The God of Abraham, Isaac, and Jacob." Exodus 3:15 and John 8:38-39 (KJV).

TEST YOUR KNOWLEDGE

Answer the following questions.

1. School of the prophets provides several things. What are two of the things they provide? _____ and _____ .

2. What is a prophet and the ministry gift of a prophet?

_____

_____

_____

3. Three things take place when you are prophesying unto others. What are those three things?

E_____

E_____

C_____

4. Do prophets often walk alone with fewer friends? ____Yes ____No.

5. What is one key thing that is important during the training process? _____.

6. There were three schools located in the communities of Bethel, Jericho, and Jordan River. These prophets were devoted to God and served God. Who did they follow the teachings of? _____, _____, and _____.

7. What does it mean to "see and behold"? _____

8. Is it uncommon for prophets to face opposition? ____Yes ____No.

9. What direction should a prophet point you in? _____.

10. There are several prophets mentioned in the Bible. Which prophet performed a miracle of provision for a widow? _____.

11. Who does the Fivefold Ministry consist of?

_____

_____

_____

_____

_____

12. How many prophets Jesus had in his inner circle that he could take to the mountain with him for transfiguration? _____.

True or False. Put a T or F in the space provided for each statement.

1. ___You can have the gift of prophecy but not walk in the office of a prophet.

2. ___ The office of a prophet holds a greater authority to gossip and walk in a greater authority and power.

3. ___ Prophets should have a life of prayer and fasting.

4. ___ Waiting is not necessarily important in the prophetic ministry.

5. ___ When God speaks, sometimes people want you to change what God is saying.

6. ___ When character is exercised *faith* is exercised.

7. ___ Prophets should not have a consecrated life.

8. ___ Prophets must be fathered by an experienced prophet.

9. ___ Where there's doubt, there will be less movement, less flow.

10. ___ True prophets have absolutely all power in and of themselves.

11. ___ Jericho: faith walk; completion, wholeness in the prophetic office.

12. ___ Prophets must be at peace with God.

13. ___ Prophecy is your imagination.

14. ___ The anointing can be transferred through distance by speaking the Word.

15. ___ Prophets should be devoted and willing to serve.

16. ___ Prophets do not have to be dedicated to the training process.

17. ___ Prophecy must edify, exhort, and comfort, NOT DESTROY.

18. ___ Gigal: triangle, stone, hard place.

19. ___ A prophet is God's spokesperson, a mouthpiece on earth.

20. ___ Every gift in the Fivefold Ministry is a power gift from God.

21. ___ Manifestation means to see and behold.

22. ___ Prophets will never face opposition.

23. ___ The Holy Spirit cannot be fabricated.

24. ___ Exhort" means to strongly discourage someone.

25. ___ You cannot do anything without the Holy Spirit.

Multiple choice questions. Circle the letter of your answer.

1. What does a mantle represent?

a. Spiritual covering
b. Cloak
c. Release of gifting
d. All the above

2. How often should a prophet pray?

a. Once a month
b. Once a week
c. Every day
d. Once a quarter

3. What did Samuel represent?

a. The air and wind of God
b. The love and kindness of God
c. The power and authority of God
d. The grace and mercy of God

4. Part of being a prophet is learning how to do what in ministry?

a. Pastor a church
b. Dance
c. Serve
d. Shout

5. What does it mean for a prophet to yield?

a. Be aggressive
b. Rebel
c. Decline
d. Submit

6. Who is not honored in their own hometown, country?

a. A prophet
b. A father
c. A leader
d. A pastor

7. Elisha not only received a double portion from Elijah. What else did he receive?

a. The ring
b. The mantle, mandate, and the mission
c. The coat of many colors
d. The title and the certificate of ordination

8. What is the doorway to receiving a revelation from God?

a. Worship
b. Singing
c. Dancing
d. Reading

9. What fivefold ministry gift is gentler than the apostle and the prophet?

a. Evangelist
b. Pastor
c. Minister
d. Teacher

10. What should God's truth be spoken in?

a. Hate
b. Strife
c. Confusion
d. Love

Fill in the blank.

1. _____ kills prophets.

2. Who did Samuel anoint to prophesy? _____.

3. The word minister means to _____, _____, _____.

4. Distractions prevent you from _____.

5. A prophet must be totally _____ to God.

6. What does the acronym SIYL stand for_____.

7. God's original garden had _____ _____ flowing out of it.

8. An example of a word curse is: _____.

9. Seek to yield to the _____.

10. It is very important to live a life of _____.

11. _____ is one thing you need to protect and preserve.

12. _____affects one's situation, circumstance, or accomplishments.

13. Bringing _____ to chaos means bringing life and _____.

14. _____declares that we will eat the good of the land if we are willing and obedient.

15. The most mature _____ doesn't have all the knowledge.

List ten things a prophet should do.

1._____

2._____

3._____

4._____

5._____

6._____

7._____

8._____

8._____

10._____

List ten things a prophet should not do.

1._____

2._____

3._____

4._____

5._____

6._____

7._____

8._____

8._____

10._____

INTERNET RESOURCES

School of the Prophets and Company of Prophets. Accessed January 15, 2015 through https://www.gotquestions.org/school-of-prophets.html and https://bible.knowing-jesus.com/phrases/Company-Of-Prophets

Sons of the Prophets. Accessed January 15, 2015 through https://biblehub.com/commentaries/pulpit/2_kings/6.htm

Blume, M.F. (1995). There is a River. The Four Rivers of Eden. Accessed January 15, 2015 through https://www.mikeblume.com/4rivers.htm

Freidzon, Claudio. (2013). How to Maintain the Flow of the Anointing. Accessed January 23, 2015 through https://www.charismamag.com/spirit/supernatural/9382-maintaining-the-flow

Character. Accessed January 23, 2015 through http://kingwatch.co.nz/Prophetic_Ministry/character.htm

Cedeno, Emil. s.d. The Prophet's Training and Maturation Process. Accessed January 23, 2015 through http://www.bloodofjesus.50megs.com/the_prophet%27s_training_and_maturation_process.htm

Warner, Sandy. s.d. He Speaks through Impartation. Acessed January 30, 2015 through http://www.thequickenedword.info/classes/WhereGodSpeaks/Touch/LessonImpartationTouches.htm

Pete Bumgarner Ministries. (1984). The Fivefold Ministry. Accessed January 30, 2015 through https://www.stcbiblecollege.com/StudyGuides/TopicalGuides/FivefoldMinistrySG.pdf

Gause, Shomari. s.d. The Origin of the FiveFold Ministry. Accessed January 30, 2015 through https://www.truthrightlydivided.com/five-fold-ministry/

MORE NOTES

www.ingramcontent.com/pod-product-compliance
Lightning Source LLC
Chambersburg PA
CBHW062053090426
42740CB00016B/3124